The Merchant Enticed by

The Pearl of Great Price

Mary Joslin * Illustrated by Meilo So

LION
Children's Books

Down by the river, the children used to play together. Rich or poor, they all joined in the same games.

To Jo & Martin N.F.

To my mother M.S.

Text by Mary Joslin
Illustrations copyright © 2000 Meilo So
Design by Nicky Farthing
This edition copyright © 2000 Lion Publishing

The moral rights of the author and illustrator
have been asserted

Published by
Lion Publishing plc
Sandy Lane West, Oxford, England
www.lion-publishing.co.uk
ISBN 0 7459 4502 3 (hardback)
ISBN 0 7459 4522 8 (paperback)

First hardback edition 2000
10 9 8 7 6 5 4 3 2 1 0
First paperback edition 2000
10 9 8 7 6 5 4 3 2 1 0

A catalogue record for this book is available
from the British Library

Typeset in 16/28 Baskerville BT
Printed and bound in Malaysia

**This Bible tale is adapted from Jesus' parable of
the Pearl of Great Price, which can be found in Matthew,
chapter 13, verses 45–46.**

One day, they went diving in the deeper pools.

'Look!' cried a boy. 'Look what I've found!'

'It's a pearl,' said another. 'It's beautiful.'

The children gathered round to look.

They were all eager to touch it, but who

would dare ask the one big question…

'Can I have it? Please. It's so lovely.'

It was a boy who spoke first.

'It really belongs to Josh. He found it,' said one of the girls.

'You can have it, Reuben,' said the one called Josh, 'because you really like it.'

From that day on, the other children saw less of Reuben. While they played outdoors, he stayed inside, reading about pearls.

When his family asked him what he wanted for a present, he always asked for a pearl. 'I shall be a pearl merchant when I grow up,' he said.

And so he was. He left the riverside town that had been his home, waving goodbye to his childhood friends.

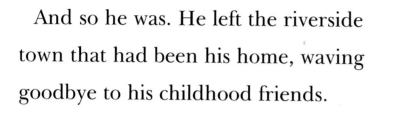

He travelled to the great city, where pearls were bought and sold. He traded some of his smaller pearls for larger, finer ones.

He travelled to the ocean shore, where
fishermen unloaded their nets, and he
searched the oyster shells for new pearls.
Most were misshapen, but now and then
he found one that was round and good.

He travelled to the lands where pearl fishers
went diving for the finest pearls—some silvery
pale, others glowing rosy pink.

So eager was he to find the very best,
he himself explored the dark green
sea; the danger was nothing
compared with the joy of
finding each new treasure.

He became a wealthy man. Other merchants
would travel anywhere in the world to meet him.

They would trade their pearls: a bag of seed
pearls for a fine large one,

three oval pearls for one that was perfectly round…

vast amounts of gold for the one exquisite tear-drop pearl

to complete a necklace for a princess.

But although Reuben was rich, he was never completely satisfied. 'Somewhere,' he said, 'there must be a pearl that is utterly perfect. I shall not stop looking until I find it.' So he travelled on, through all the world.

At last, he came once again to the place
where he had grown up.

'Reuben!' called a voice. 'It's good to see you.'
He turned to see Josh, playing with the children
down by the river.

'Look what we've just found,' said Josh.
Reuben's childhood friend held up a pearl.
'Isn't it beautiful?' said the children. 'Do you
think it's worth anything?'
'I imagine it's worth a very great deal,'
said Reuben, gazing at it reverently.
'It's the finest pearl I've ever seen.
It's… quite perfect. Can I buy it? Please.'
'It really belongs to Josh. He found
it,' said one of the girls.

'Of course, I'll pay whatever you like,' said Reuben.
'It's up to you,' replied Josh. 'If this is the pearl
you want most in all the world, you must decide
what you're prepared to give for it.'
'Everything,' replied Reuben.

And so he did,
amidst great
celebration.